A Fragrant Offering

A Daily Prayer Cycle in the Celtic Tradition

John Birch

Dedication

To all those who have learned to see within the beauty of a Butterfly's wing the brushstrokes of the Creator.

Contents

1   Introduction   1

2   Sunday   4

3   Monday   15

4   Tuesday   26

5   Wednesday   37

6   Thursday   48

7   Friday   59

8   Saturday   70

9   Celtic Festivals   81

10   Celtic Blessings   108

  References   110

  About the Author   111

A Heritage of Prayer

Alone with none but thee, my God,
I journey on my way.
What need I fear, when thou art near,
O king of night and day?
More safe am I within thy hand
Than if a host did round me stand.
(Columba, c.521 - 97)

I arise today
Through a mighty strength:
God's power to guide me,
God's might to uphold me,
God's eyes to watch over me;
God's ear to hear me,
God's word to give me speech,
God's hand to guard me,
God's way to lie before me,
God's shield to shelter me,
God's host to secure me.
(first millenium - Brigid of Gael).

Introduction

"Evening, morning and noon I cry out in distress, and he hears my voice."
(Psalm 55:17)

The earliest pattern we have of regular Christian daily prayer, other than that in the New Testament comes from the Didache (or Teaching of the Twelve Apostles) which was probably written at the end of the first century. It states that the Lord's Prayer should be said three times a day, but does not say at which times. During the early development of the Christian Church, a pattern of praying at the third, sixth and ninth hour of the day became established (with arguments from Scripture). Origen, in the third century recommended another session or prayer in the evening.

This was the pattern used (with variation) both by desert monks and their followers, and the ordinary urban or rural Christians. One spiritual argument for a threefold prayer cycle was that the Holy Spirit descended on the apostle at the third hour (9 a.m.), Peter had his famous vision that led him to the acceptance of Gentiles into the Church at the sixth hour (noon), and was going to the temple with John at the ninth hour when he met the paralyzed man at the gate to the temple. The angel also appeared to the centurion Cornelius at the ninth hour (3 p.m.)

1

It is likely that some rural communities followed the natural rhythm of the day, praying morning, noon and evening (their lives determined by the movements of the sun), whilst others in the towns kept more strictly to the third, sixth and ninth hours.

Christians viewed their commitment to prayer as a daily sacrifice which was a spiritual fulfilment of the Old Testament sacrifices.

By the fourth century the Church was praying together more often than individually, led by Bishops, Priests and Deacons. Along with the prayers are found psalms and hymns, with Psalms 148-150 often associated with morning prayers each day and Psalm 141 in the evening.

We have to remember that very few Christians would have access to the printed Word of God, and therefore the psalms were learned by heart and meditated upon, as within them it was considered lay much of the truth of the Scriptures and prophesy concerning Christ. Particularly devout monks learned the entire canon of psalms and even recited them all within a 24 hour period.

St Basil says of the psalms that they "prophesy what is to come, recall history, legislate for life, give practical advice and are a treasury of good teaching."

The form of liturgy used in public worship by this time focused mainly on prayer and intercession, with little emphasis on confession of sins. However, in the deserts of Egypt and Syria the monastic movements that were growing up had a strong penitential emphasis, and it is likely that bishops who spent time within these communities took back to their churches this same penitential approach to prayer for all Christians.

Basil of Caesarea in his Longer Rules advises confession not only for what has been done, but also for what has not been done.

I have tried to keep to a simple mix of prayer and scripture similar to the pattern used in the very earliest Christian communities, using familiar themes relating to the journey of humankind's relationship with their God.

Throughout the liturgies are opportunities for sharing the reading of both prayer and scripture (if that is helpful).

In the morning prayers I have included confession and on alternate days a sharing of the peace - a more modern version of the ancient 'kiss of peace' practiced by the early church, though feel free to share a hug as well as a hand!

Where the Lord's Prayer is used, I have included the version found in Matthew's Gospel, but you may wish to use the one you are familiar with.

For the midday prayers I have adapted the ancient practice of *Lectio Divina*, which is a slow, contemplative prayerful reading of a portion of Scripture, allowing it to speak directly to our hearts and lives. This method of praying is particularly loved by the Benedictine tradition of monasticism. St. Benedict encourages us to hear Scripture's words with "the ear of our hearts" and hear that "gentle whisper" that Elijah heard on the mountain. Fr. Luke Dysinger, O.S.B.*, whose notes on the subject I have followed and adapted, describes *Lectio Divina* as "reverential listening; listening both in a spirit of silence and of awe."

The pattern followed is that of Reading (or listening), Meditation, Prayer and Contemplation. I have allowed for both individual and group participation in this method of praying. For this study I have used Psalms as our guide through the week, but feel free to use whichever Scripture passage seems appropriate – perhaps work through part of a Gospel or use appointed readings for the day.

Because the early church was involved in mission and evangelism within a pagan culture, I have also added some of the familiar Celtic/Pagan festivals to this collection, particularly where the church has not already Christianized these with suitable liturgies. Most of these involve the natural world, the cycle of seasons and the all-important sowing and harvesting of crops. As such, they are within our appreciation of God's world and worthy of our praise!

*http://www.valyermo.com/ld-art.html.

Sunday Morning – The gift of a world

(* Indicates optional change of reader. Bold text to be read by all)

We meet in the name of Father,
Son and Holy Spirit
within this precious time and place.
We meet as would a family,
bound as one together
in love, within this sacred space.

God of peace and unity
be in our arriving and departing.

*God of love and family
be in our meeting and welcoming.

*God of truth and mercy
be in our reading and understanding.

*God of hope and prophesy
be in our hearing and following.

Psalm 145 (vs. 1-7)

(As you read and listen, use the pauses to let the words speak to your hearts)

I will exalt you, my God the King;
I will praise your name for ever and ever.

*Every day I will praise you
and extol your name forever and ever.

4

Great is the Lord and most worthy of praise;
his greatness no one can fathom.
One generation commends your works to another;
they tell of your mighty acts.

(PAUSE)

*They speak of the glorious splendor of your majesty –
and I will meditate on your wonderful works.
They tell of the power of your awesome works –
and I will proclaim your great deeds.
They celebrate your abundant goodness
and joyfully sing of your righteousness.

I will exalt you, my God the King;
I will praise your name for ever and ever

**Glory to the Father,
and to the Son,
and to the Holy Spirit,
Three in One. Amen**

In the light of God's glory our hearts lie exposed,
revealing the sin within.

**For that which we ought to have done,
to bring a blessing
or word in due season,
forgive us, gracious Lord.
For that which we have already done,
which has caused a wound
or moved someone to anger,
forgive us, gracious Lord.
May these be lives that are devoted
to serving you, and all
whom you would lead us to.**

If we, in humility, will confess our sins
in the quietness of our hearts or in the company of the
faithful, God's love and mercy bring forgiveness.

Let us share the peace of Christ Jesus with those around us.

'Peace I leave with you,' said Jesus. 'My peace I give you.'
'Again Jesus said, "Peace be with you!"'

(Pause while the peace is shared)

Give thanks to the Lord, for he is good;
His love endures forever

Genesis 1:27-30

So God created mankind in his own image, in the image of God he created them; male and female he created them. God blessed them and said to them, "Be fruitful and increase in number; fill the earth and subdue it. Rule over the fish in the sea and the birds in the sky and over every living creature that moves on the ground."

(PAUSE)

Then God said, "I give you every seed-bearing plant on the face of the whole earth and every tree that has fruit with seed in it. They will be yours for food. And to all the beasts of the earth and all the birds in the sky and all the creatures that move along the ground – everything that has the breath of life in it – I give every green plant for food." And it was so.

For the wonder of Creation,
which is such a precious gift
We will sing your praise

For the image of the divine
imprinted in our hearts
We will sing your praise

For the joy of community
and the blessing that it gives
We will sing your praise

Matthew 6:9-13

> **Our Father in heaven,**
> **hallowed be your name,**
> **your kingdom come,**
> **your will be done,**
> **on earth as it is in heaven.**
> **Give us today our daily bread.**
> **And forgive us our debts,**
> **as we also have forgiven our debtors.**
> **And lead us not into temptation,**
> **but deliver us from the evil one. Amen**

May this be a day of hope,
of expectation,
relishing each moment
as a gift from you.

May this be a day of freedom,
of breaking free,
loosening the chains that
still surround us.

May this be a day of peace,
of wholeness,
knowing that our lives
are in your hands.

May this be a day of joy,
of blessing,

living in your kingdom
as a child of God.
Amen

Now the majesty of God
bring our hearts to rejoicing,
the Spirit's breath
fill our souls to overflowing,
and the grace of God
lead our hands to serving,
this day and all days.
Amen.

Sunday Midday – Lectio Divina

(Individual or small group)

This is slight variation on an ancient technique of contemplative prayer, which helps us to connect our hearts with the Word of God. It has been kept alive particularly within the Benedictine monastic tradition. It requires that we allow for quietness in the bustle of the day, to listen for the 'gentle whisper' of God. These studies use the Psalms, but any suitable passage (preferably not too long) may be used.

Lectio - Reading

Read twice, slowly and attentively, listening for that 'gentle whisper' that is God's word or phrase for today, using this or an alternative reading.

> Blessed are those whose help is the God of Jacob,
> whose hope is in the Lord their God.
> He is the Maker of heaven and earth,
> the sea, and everything in them –
> he remains faithful for ever.
> He upholds the cause of the oppressed
> and gives food to the hungry.
> The Lord sets prisoners free,
> the Lord gives sight to the blind,
> the Lord lifts up those who are bowed down,
> the Lord loves the righteous.
> The Lord watches over the foreigner
> and sustains the fatherless and the widow,
> but he frustrates the ways of the wicked.
> *(Psalm 146:5-9)*

Meditatio – Meditation (2-3 min)

As Mary 'pondered in her heart' what she heard and saw of Jesus, so we repeat these words silently and let them sink into our hearts, interact with our day, our thoughts and concerns… God's word becomes our word for today.

(Group – allow time for those who wish to share the word, image or phrase that has touched their heart.)

Oratio - Prayer

As we turn to prayer, so God invites us to respond to the word or phrase that has spoken to us. In the quietness or aloud we bring to Him those words, images or people that God has placed on our hearts, and how we might put those words into action.

(Group – allow time to pray for the person on your right.)

Contemplatio – Contemplation

We spend a minute or two in silence, enjoying the experience of God's presence and love embracing us

> **Glory to the Father,**
> **and to the Son,**
> **and to the Holy Spirit,**
> **Three in One.**
> **Amen.**

Sunday Evening

(* Indicates optional change of reader. Bold text to be read by all)

Lord of all we see,
Lord of all we hear,
Lord of all we sense,
Lord of all we are,
to you we bring
this offering of prayer.

In the quiet of this moment,
this precious moment.
Hear our prayer

*In the presence of your Spirit,
your precious Spirit.
Hear our prayer

*In the company of this people,
this precious people.
Hear our prayer

Psalm 19:1-6

(As you read and listen, use the pauses to let the words speak to your hearts)

The heavens declare the glory of God;
the skies proclaim the work of his hands.

Day after day they pour forth speech;
night after night they reveal knowledge.
They have no speech, they use no words;
no sound is heard from them.
Yet their voice goes out into all the earth,

their words to the ends of the world.

(PAUSE)

*In the heavens God has pitched a tent for the sun.
It is like a bridegroom coming out of his chamber,
like a champion rejoicing to run his course. It rises
at one end of the heavens and makes its circuit
to the other; nothing is deprived of its warmth

The heavens declare the glory of God;
the skies proclaim the work of his hands.

Glory to the Father,
and to the Son,
and to the Holy Spirit,
Three in One.
Amen

2 Corinthians 6:16b-18

As God has said: "I will live with them and walk among them, and
I will be their God, and they will be my people."
"Therefore, come out from them and be separate, says the Lord.
Touch no unclean thing, and I will receive you."
"I will be a Father to you, and you will be my sons and daughters,
says the Lord Almighty."

John 1:9-13

*The true light that gives light to everyone was coming into the
world. He was in the world, and though the world was made
through him, the world did not recognize him. He came to that
which was his own, but his own did not receive him. Yet to all who
did receive him, to those who believed in his name, he gave the
right to become children of God – children born not of natural
descent, nor of human decision or a husband's will, but born of
God.

(PAUSE)

For the privilege of prayer,
our hearts reaching out,
touching the divine.
Word of Life, speak to us.

*For the privilege of service,
our lives reaching out,
letting your light shine.
Word of Life, speak through us.

Matthew 6:9-13

Our Father in heaven,
hallowed be your name,
your kingdom come,
your will be done,
on earth as it is in heaven.
Give us today our daily bread.
And forgive us our debts,
as we also have forgiven our debtors.
And lead us not into temptation,
but deliver us from the evil one.
Amen.

For those who have no faith
Embrace them, Lord, we pray

For those who have no hope
Embrace them, Lord, we pray
For those struggling to cope
Embrace them, Lord, we pray

For those who are alone
Embrace them, Lord, we pray,
using these arms
and these voices
if that should be your will.
Amen

As one day draws to a close
and heralds in dawn's fresh light,
may the blessing our hearts have received
be the blessing our hearts proclaim
at the moment that we wake.

Now may the God of love
keep us safe in his arms,
the God of peace
bring to us sweet rest,
and the God of joy
let us wake refreshed.
Amen

Monday Morning – A community of faith

May the unity of the Godhead,
Father, Son and Spirit
be at the center of our meeting
and bind these hearts as one.

Bless the Lord, O my soul
And all that is within us,
bless the Lord,
bless the Lord!

For this community of faith
Surround us in your love

For those unable to be here
Surround them in your love

For all who turn to you in prayer
Surround them in your love

Psalm 96:1-6

(As you read and listen, use the pauses to let the words speak to your hearts)

Sing to the Lord a new song;
sing to the Lord, all the earth.

*Sing to the Lord, praise his name;
proclaim his salvation day after day.

Declare his glory among the nations,
his marvelous deeds among all peoples.
For great is the Lord and most worthy of praise;
he is to be feared above all gods.

(PAUSE)

*For all the gods of the nations are idols,
but the Lord made the heavens.
Splendor and majesty are before him;
strength and glory are in his sanctuary

Sing to the Lord a new song;
sing to the Lord, all the earth.

**Glory to the Father,
and to the Son,
and to the Holy Spirit,
Three in One.
Amen.**

For Truth that speaks to hearts
Lord, show us your mercy

*For grace beyond imagining
Lord, show us your mercy

*For forgiveness from our sin
Lord, show us your mercy

You have given us each other,
that through this community of faith
others might be drawn to you.
Forgive us when, through lack of love
these lives do not reflect your grace
and our words bring anything but peace.
May this place bring a blessing
to all who enter, and this people
become the face of Christ
that they shall see today.

Lord, in your mercy
Hear our prayer

If we confess our sins, he is faithful and just and will forgive
us our sins, and purify us from all unrighteousness.

Exodus 33:12-17

Moses said to the Lord, "You have been telling me, 'Lead these
people,' but you have not let me know whom you will send with
me. You have said, 'I know you by name and you have found favor
with me.' If you are pleased with me, teach me your ways so I may
know you and continue to find favor with you. Remember that this
nation is your people."

(PAUSE)

*The Lord replied, "My Presence will go with you, and I will give
you rest."
Then Moses said to him, "If your Presence does not go with us, do
not send us up from here. How will anyone know that you are
pleased with me and with your people unless you go with us?
What else will distinguish me and your people from all the other
people on the face of the earth?"
And the Lord said to Moses, "I will do the very thing you have
asked, because I am pleased with you and I know you by name."

(PAUSE)

*For your people, wherever they might gather
Be the one who stands beside

*For your people, wherever they might journey
Be the one who is our guide

*For your people, wherever they might suffer
Be the one who keeps us safe

*For your people, wherever they might struggle
Be the one who gives us strength

Matthew 6:9-13

> **Our Father in heaven,**
> **hallowed be your name,**
> **your kingdom come,**
> **your will be done,**
> **on earth as it is in heaven.**
> **Give us today our daily bread.**
> **And forgive us our debts,**
> **as we also have forgiven our debtors.**
> **And lead us not into temptation,**
> **but deliver us from the evil one.**
> **Amen.**

God who calls us
from wilderness places
into sacred spaces and green pastures
that you have prepared for us
To you belongs our praise

*God who calls us
into difficult places
and to darker spaces where our trust
is in the strength that you provide
To you belongs our praise

*God who calls us, leads us,
guides and shields us,
To you belongs our praise

Now may God's blessing go with us,
God's love surround us,
God's footsteps guide us
and God's strength supply us
throughout the day ahead.

Monday Midday – Lectio Divina

(Individual or small group)

This is slight variation on an ancient technique of contemplative prayer, which helps us to connect our hearts with the Word of God. It has been kept alive particularly within the Benedictine monastic tradition. It requires that we allow for quietness in the bustle of the day, to listen for the 'gentle whisper' of God. These studies use the Psalms, but any suitable passage (preferably not too long) may be used.

Lectio - Reading

Read twice, slowly and attentively, listening for that 'gentle whisper' that is God's word or phrase for today, using this or an alternative reading.

> The Lord reigns for ever;
> he has established his throne for judgment.
> He rules the world in righteousness
> and judges the peoples with equity.
> The Lord is a refuge for the oppressed,
> a stronghold in times of trouble.
> Those who know your name trust in you,
> for you, Lord, have never forsaken those who seek you.
> *(Psalm 9:7-10)*

Meditatio – Meditation (2-3 min)

As Mary 'pondered in her heart' what she heard and saw of Jesus, so we repeat these words silently and let them sink into our hearts, interact with our day, our thoughts and concerns… God's word becomes our word for today.

(Group – allow time for those who wish to share the word, image or phrase that has touched their heart.)

Oratio - Prayer

As we turn to prayer, so God invites us to respond to the word or phrase that has spoken to us. In the quietness or aloud we bring to Him those words, images or people that God has placed on our hearts, and how we might put those words into action.

(Group – allow time to pray for the person on your right.)

Contemplatio – Contemplation

We spend a minute or two in silence, enjoying the experience of God's presence and love embracing us

> **Glory to the Father,**
> **and to the Son,**
> **and to the Holy Spirit,**
> **Three in One.**
> **Amen**

Monday Evening

(* Indicates optional change of reader. Bold text to be read by all)

In the name of the Father,
Son and Holy Spirit,
Three in One,
our spirits are joined
in unity with the worldwide
community of faith.

God, who in love creates us
Come, fill our lives anew

God, who in love enfolds us
Come, fill our lives anew

God, who in love sustains us
Come, fill our lives anew

God, who in love directs us
Come, fill our lives anew

God, who in love renews us
Come, fill our lives anew

Psalm 100

(As you read and listen, use the pauses to let the words speak to your hearts)

Shout for joy to the Lord, all the earth.
Worship the Lord with gladness

*Come before him with joyful songs.
Know that the Lord is God.
It is he who made us, and we are his;
we are his people, the sheep of his pasture.

(PAUSE)

*Enter his gates with thanksgiving
and his courts with praise;
give thanks to him and praise his name.
For the Lord is good and his love endures forever;
his faithfulness continues through all generations.

*Shout for joy to the Lord, all the earth.
Worship the Lord with gladness

**Glory to the Father,
and to the Son,
and to the Holy Spirit,
Three in One.
Amen**

1 John 5:1-2

Everyone who believes that Jesus is the Christ is born of God, and everyone who loves the father loves his child as well. This is how we know that we love the children of God: by loving God and carrying out his commands.

John 6:35-39

*Then Jesus declared, "I am the bread of life. Whoever comes to me will never go hungry, and whoever believes in me will never be thirsty. But as I told you, you have seen me and still you do not believe. All those the Father gives me will come to me, and whoever comes to me I will never drive away. For I have come down from heaven not to do my will but to do the will of him who sent me. And this is the will of him who sent me, that I shall lose none of all those he has given me, but raise them up at the last day."

Where there is hunger
for the Gospel to be received
Lord, have mercy.

*Where there is a thirst
for righteousness to be revealed
Lord, have mercy.

*Where there is hurting
and no one asks the question why
Lord, have mercy.

*Where there is blindness
to the suffering of this world
Lord, have mercy.

Matthew 6:9-13

**Our Father in heaven,
hallowed be your name,
your kingdom come,
your will be done,
on earth as it is in heaven.
Give us today our daily bread.
And forgive us our debts,
as we also have forgiven our debtors.
And lead us not into temptation,
but deliver us from the evil one.
Amen.**

For this day of possibilities;
the roads that we have walked,
glances and greetings exchanged,
conversations and silences,
decisions made or deferred,

successes and failures,
prayers whispered or left unsaid,
blessings given or received;
for this day of possibilities
and the one that is to come
we give to you our thanks.

Now may the God of love surround us,
the God of love protect us,
the God of love bring us safe
through this night, and all nights,
the God of love bring us awake
once more to dawn's fresh light.

Tuesday Morning – Journeying together

(* Indicates optional change of reader. Bold text to be read by all)

In the unity of Father,
Son and Holy Spirit
these hearts are joined as one

You who are in our beginning
and our ending,
and the journeying between,
be with us in this time of refreshment,
an oasis in the day,
and feed us with your word.

*You who are at our departing
and arriving,
and everything that is seen,
be with us as, eyes open, we marvel
at all that you have made,
and fill our hearts with praise.

Psalm 148:7-14

(As you read and listen, use the pauses to let the words speak to your hearts)

Praise the Lord from the heavens
Praise him in the heights above

*Praise the Lord from the earth,
you great sea creatures and all ocean depths,
lightning and hail, snow and clouds,
stormy winds that do his bidding,

(PAUSE)

*you mountains and all hills,
fruit trees and all cedars,
wild animals and all cattle,
small creatures and flying birds,
kings of the earth and all nations,
you princes and all rulers on earth,
young men and women,
old men and children.
Let them praise the name of the Lord,

(PAUSE)

*for his name alone is exalted;
his splendor is above the earth and the heavens.
And he has raised up for his people a horn,
the praise of all his faithful servants,
of Israel, the people close to his heart.

Praise the Lord from the heavens
Praise him in the heights above

**Glory to the Father,
and to the Son,
and to the Holy Spirit,
Three in One.
Amen**

For Truth that speaks to hearts
Lord, show us your mercy

*For grace beyond imagining
Lord, show us your mercy

*For forgiveness from our sin
Lord, show us your mercy

Lord, you call us to be different
as we journey through this day,
to be a guide to those who wander,
offer help and seek the lost.
Forgive us when we fail to become
the people we should be.

*Lord, you call us to be different
in the ebb and flow of life,
to see the good in all your children,
demonstrate your love and grace.
Forgive us when we fail to become
the people we should be.

*Lord, you call!
Equip and strengthen
your people for the task,
that within our daily journeying
we might bless the lives we meet.
Amen

If we, in humility, will confess our sins
in the quietness of our hearts or in the company of the
faithful, God's love and mercy bring forgiveness.

Let us share the peace of Christ Jesus with those around us.

'Peace I leave with you,' said Jesus. 'My peace I give you.'
'Again Jesus said, "Peace be with you!"'

(Pause while the peace is shared)

Give thanks to the Lord, for he is good;
His love endures forever

Isaiah 40:28-31

*Do you not know? Have you not heard? The LORD is the everlasting God, the Creator of the ends of the earth. He will not grow tired or weary, and his understanding no one can fathom.

(PAUSE)

*He gives strength to the weary and increases the power of the weak. Even youths grow tired and weary, and young men stumble and fall; but those who hope in the LORD will renew their strength. They will soar on wings like eagles; they will run and not grow weary, they will walk and not be faint.

Matthew 6:9-13

> **Our Father in heaven,**
> **hallowed be your name,**
> **your kingdom come,**
> **your will be done,**
> **on earth as it is in heaven.**
> **Give us today our daily bread.**
> **And forgive us our debts,**
> **as we also have forgiven our debtors.**
> **And lead us not into temptation,**
> **but deliver us from the evil one.**
> **Amen.**

God of morning and rising sun,
with breaking dawn the beauty
of your creativity
is revealed for all to see.
And we shall sing your praise.

*God of noontime and gentle rain,
you bring to us refreshment
on our daily journeying,
and the strength to persevere.
And we shall sing your praise.

*God of evening and setting sun,
you send us out in faith
and bring us safely home again,
such is your love and grace.
And we shall sing your praise.

Now may the hand of God go with us
on our journeying today,
the love of God surround us
as we venture on our way,
the Spirit of God be present
in everything we say
and God's blessing be the gift
that we freely give away.

Tuesday Midday – Lectio Divina

(Individual or small group)

This is slight variation on an ancient technique of contemplative prayer, which helps us to connect our hearts with the Word of God. It has been kept alive particularly within the Benedictine monastic tradition. It requires that we allow for quietness in the bustle of the day, to listen for the 'gentle whisper' of God. These studies use the Psalms, but any suitable passage (preferably not too long) may be used.

Lectio - Reading

Read twice, slowly and attentively, listening for that 'gentle whisper' that is God's word or phrase for today, using this or an alternative reading.

> The earth is the Lord's, and everything in it,
> the world, and all who live in it;
> for he founded it on the seas
> and established it on the waters.
> Who may ascend the mountain of the Lord?
> Who may stand in his holy place?
> The one who has clean hands and a pure heart,
> who does not trust in an idol
> or swear by a false god.
> They will receive blessing from the Lord
> and vindication from God their Saviour.

Such is the generation of those who seek him,
who seek your face, God of Jacob.
(Psalm 24:1-6)

Meditatio – Meditation (2-3 min)

As Mary 'pondered in her heart' what she heard and saw of Jesus,
so we repeat these words silently and let them sink into our hearts,
interact with our day, our thoughts and concerns… God's word
becomes our word for today.

*(Group – allow time for those who wish to share the word, image or phrase that
has touched their heart.)*

Oratio - Prayer

As we turn to prayer, so God invites us to respond to the word or
phrase that has spoken to us. In the quietness or aloud we bring to
Him those words, images or people that God has placed on our
hearts, and how we might put those words into action.

(Group – allow time to pray for the person on your right.)

Contemplatio – Contemplation

We spend a minute or two in silence, enjoying the experience of
God's presence and love embracing us

Glory to the Father,
and to the Son,
and to the Holy Spirit,
Three in One.
Amen

Tuesday Evening

(* Indicates optional change of reader. Bold text to be read by all)

In the presence of Father,
Son and Holy Spirit,
Blesséd Trinity,
we meet with gratitude,
in quietness and reflection
at the closing of this day.
Bless the road that we have travelled
and those we met along the way.
Hear us Lord, we pray

Bless the glances we exchanged,
the prayers and words we shared today.
Hear us Lord, we pray

Psalm 139:1-8

(As you read and listen, use the pauses to let the words speak to your hearts)

You have searched me, Lord,
and you know me.

You know when I sit and when I rise;
you perceive my thoughts from afar.
You discern my going out and my lying down;
you are familiar with all my ways.
Before a word is on my tongue
you, Lord, know it completely.

(PAUSE)

*You hem me in behind and before,
and you lay your hand upon me.
Such knowledge is too wonderful for me,
too lofty for me to attain.
Where can I go from your Spirit?
Where can I flee from your presence?
If I go up to the heavens, you are there;
if I make my bed in the depths, you are there.

You have searched me, Lord,
  and you know me.

**Glory to the Father,
and to the Son,
and to the Holy Spirit,
Three in One.
Amen**

Acts 16:6-12

*Paul and his companions travelled throughout the region of
Phrygia and Galatia, having been kept by the Holy Spirit from
preaching the word in the province of Asia. When they came to the
border of Mysia, they tried to enter Bithynia, but the Spirit of Jesus
would not allow them to.

(PAUSE)

*So they passed by Mysia and went down to Troas. During the
night Paul had a vision of a man of Macedonia standing and
begging him, "Come over to Macedonia and help us." After Paul
had seen the vision, we got ready at once to leave for Macedonia,
concluding that God had called us to preach the gospel to them.

Matthew 15:29-30

*Jesus left there and went along the Sea of Galilee. Then he went up on a mountainside and sat down. Great crowds came to him, bringing the lame, the blind, the crippled, the mute and many others, and laid them at his feet; and he healed them.

(PAUSE)

For each step that we might take
Be our guide, O Lord of life.

For each load that we might bear
Be our strength, O Lord of life.

For each mountain we might face
Be our power, O Lord of life.

For each river that might impede
Be our safety, O Lord of life.

For each place where we might rest
Be our peace, O Lord of life.

For each sunrise and sunset
Be our joy, O Lord of life.

Matthew 6:9-13

Our Father in heaven,
hallowed be your name,
your kingdom come,
your will be done,
on earth as it is in heaven.
Give us today our daily bread.
And forgive us our debts,
as we also have forgiven our debtors.
And lead us not into temptation,
 but deliver us from the evil one.
Amen.

For those whose spiritual journey
is really only just beginning.
Bless them, Lord, we pray.

*For all whose journey of faith
is beset by doubt and uncertainty
Bless them, Lord, we pray.

*For those whose daily journey
is hindered by pain or suffering
Bless them, Lord, we pray.

*For those who spend their journey
helping others struggling on the road
Bless them, Lord, we pray.

Let our eyes be your eyes,
sharing compassion, warmth and love.
Let our hands be your hands
bringing healing with their touch.
Let our ears be your ears
listening where there is need.
Let our words be your words
bringing comfort joy and peace

God of the morning,
be with us as we rise,
God of the noontime,
be with us in our walk,
God of the evening,
be with us as we rest.

Wednesday Morning – from desert places

We meet in the name
of our Creator,
Savior, and Sustainer.
We meet as one
with the Three in One,
Father, Son and Spirit.

The Lord is here!
We rest in his embrace.

The Lord is here!
And in our hearts forever!

God of grace and mercy,
present both in desert places
and green pastures,
who knows the shadows
in which we wander
and longs for us to walk in light,
whose arms embrace all those
who in despair cry out.
To you alone belongs our praise!

*God of grace and mercy,
who knows the people we could be
yet loves us as we are.
To you alone belongs our praise!

*God of grace and mercy,
who understands our frailty
and hears us when we call.
To you alone belongs our praise!

Psalm 62:1,5-8,11-12a

(As you read and listen, use the pauses to let the words speak to your hearts)

Truly my soul finds rest in God;
my salvation comes from him.

Yes, my soul, find rest in God;
my hope comes from him.
Truly he is my rock and my salvation;
he is my fortress, I shall not be shaken.
My salvation and my honor depend on God;
he is my mighty rock, my refuge.
Trust in him at all times, you people;
pour out your hearts to him,
 for God is our refuge.

(PAUSE)

*One thing God has spoken,
two things I have heard:
'Power belongs to you, God,
and with you, Lord, is unfailing love'

Truly my soul finds rest in God;
my salvation comes from him.

Glory to the Father,
and to the Son,
and to the Holy Spirit,
Three in One.
Amen

In the light of God's glory our hearts lie exposed,
revealing the sin within.

Gracious God, who reaches out
to those who stumble,
embraces the humble,
seeks the lost,
forgive us when we lose our way.
Take us in your arms
and bring us home again,
that we might daily know your presence
and in our lives reflect your grace.
Amen

Scripture tells us that for those who confess their sins,
the Lord our God is merciful and forgiving.

Isaiah 49:13-16a

Shout for joy, you heavens;
rejoice, you earth;
burst into song, you mountains!
For the Lord comforts his people
and will have compassion on his afflicted ones.

But Zion said, "The Lord has forsaken me,
the Lord has forgotten me."

*"Can a mother forget the baby at her breast
and have no compassion on the child she has borne?
Though she may forget, I will not forget you!
See, I have engraved you on the palms of my hands..."

(PAUSE)

Speak to our hearts, Lord,
that our hearts might speak of you.
Speak to our minds, Lord,
that our words might speak of you.

Speak to our souls, Lord
that our lives might shine for you.

You are the shepherd
who walks the extra mile
to find the sheep that is lost.
Such is your love for us.

*You are the merchant
who sold all that he had
to buy a pearl of great price.
Such is your love for us.

*You are the farmer
who sows in fertile soil,
anticipating harvest.
Such is your love for us.

*You are the outsider
who does not cross the road
but stops to help a stranger.
Such is your love for us.

Matthew 6:9-13

Our Father in heaven,
hallowed be your name,
your kingdom come,
your will be done,
on earth as it is in heaven.
Give us today our daily bread.
And forgive us our debts,
as we also have forgiven our debtors.
And lead us not into temptation,
 but deliver us from the evil one.
Amen

May the God of grace
lift you from where you are
and raise you onto higher ground.

May the God of peace
still the anguish of your soul
and bring you to a quiet place.

May the God of love
who warms our fragile hearts
be the strength you find today.

Wednesday Midday - Lectio Divina

(Individual or small group)

This is slight variation on an ancient technique of contemplative prayer, which helps us to connect our hearts with the Word of God. It has been kept alive particularly within the Benedictine monastic tradition. It requires that we allow for quietness in the bustle of the day, to listen for the 'gentle whisper' of God. These studies use the Psalms, but any suitable passage (preferably not too long) may be used.

Lectio - Reading

Read twice, slowly and attentively, listening for that 'gentle whisper' that is God's word or phrase for today, using this or an alternative reading.

> One thing I ask from the Lord,
> this only do I seek:
> that I may dwell in the house of the Lord
> all the days of my life,
> to gaze on the beauty of the Lord
> and to seek him in his temple.
> For in the day of trouble
> he will keep me safe in his dwelling;
> he will hide me in the shelter of his sacred tent
> and set me high upon a rock...
> Hear my voice when I call, Lord;
> be merciful to me and answer me.
> My heart says of you, 'Seek his face!'
> Your face, Lord, I will seek.
> *(Psalm 27:4,5,7,8)*

Meditatio – Meditation (2-3 min)

As Mary 'pondered in her heart' what she heard and saw of Jesus, so we repeat these words silently and let them sink into our hearts, interact with our day, our thoughts and concerns... God's word becomes our word for today.

(Group – allow time for those who wish to share the word, image or phrase that has touched their heart.)

Oratio - Prayer

As we turn to prayer, so God invites us to respond to the word or phrase that has spoken to us. In the quietness or aloud we bring to Him those words, images or people that God has placed on our hearts, and how we might put those words into action.

(Group – allow time to pray for the person on your right.)

Contemplatio – Contemplation

We spend a minute or two in silence, enjoying the experience of God's presence and love embracing us

> **Glory to the Father,**
> **and to the Son,**
> **and to the Holy Spirit,**
> **Three in One.**
> **Amen**

Wednesday Evening

(* Indicates optional change of reader. Bold text to be read by all)

In the quiet of evening
may our God be with us,
his Spirit fill us
and the unity of the Godhead
be the bond between us.

The Lord God is here
His presence with us

Let our hearts be warmed
His grace within us

Let our spirits soar
His love inspire us

Psalm 40:1-3

(As you read and listen, use the pauses to let the words speak to your hearts)

I waited patiently for the Lord;
he turned to me and heard my cry.

*He lifted me out of the slimy pit,
out of the mud and mire;
he set my feet on a rock
and gave me a firm place to stand.

(PAUSE)

*He put a new song in my mouth,
a hymn of praise to our God.
Many will see and fear the Lord
and put their trust in him.

*I waited patiently for the Lord;
he turned to me and heard my cry.

**Glory to the Father,
and to the Son,
and to the Holy Spirit,
Three in One. Amen**

Ephesians 3:16-18

I pray that out of his glorious riches he may strengthen you with power through his Spirit in your inner being, so that Christ may dwell in your hearts through faith. And I pray that you, being rooted and established in love, may have power, together with all the Lord's holy people, to grasp how wide and long and high and deep is the love of Christ

(PAUSE)

Matthew 11:28-30

*Come to me, all you who are weary and burdened, and I will give you rest. Take my yoke upon you and learn from me, for I am gentle and humble in heart, and you will find rest for your souls. For my yoke is easy and my burden is light.

(PAUSE)

God, who graciously brings us
through troubled times
and desert places
Embrace us with your love

*God, whose Spirit fills us,
who lifts the weak
to higher places
Embrace us with your love

*God, who patiently leads us
through well-known and
challenging places
Embrace us with your love

Matthew 6:9-13

**Our Father in heaven,
hallowed be your name,
your kingdom come,
your will be done,
on earth as it is in heaven.
Give us today our daily bread.
And forgive us our debts,
as we also have forgiven our debtors.
And lead us not into temptation,
but deliver us from the evil one.
Amen**

For a world gifted to us that it might be shared in love
Gracious Lord, we lift up your name

*For all who hunger through lack of food or prejudice
Gracious Lord, have mercy

*For all who thirst through lack of water or injustice
Gracious Lord, have mercy

*For all who suffer through illness or infirmity
Gracious Lord, have mercy

*For all who wander for lack of home or stability
Gracious Lord, have mercy

For a world gifted to us that it might be shared in love
Gracious Lord, we lift up your name

As this day draws to a close
we bring to your feet
those whose lives touched ours
just for a moment.
For smiles exchanged,
hasty greetings,
brief encounters
with people we may not know
but who are precious in your sight.
Bless these moments,
and may all such encounters
scatter a seed of your love
into the fertile earth of each day.
Amen

May we never walk
in solitude or fear,
but the fellowship
of the Spirit
warm our hearts,
the love of the Savior
bring us joy
and the shelter
of the Father's arms
forever keep us safe.

Thursday Morning – Led to a pleasant land

(* Indicates optional change of reader. Bold text to be read by all)

In the name of Father,
Son and Holy Spirit,
we meet within the unity
of the Three in One,
Blesséd Trinity.

God in our waking
Bless the day that lies ahead.

God in our walking
Bless the streets through which we tread.

God in our meeting
Bless all those to whom we're led.

God in our speaking
Bless the words that will be said.

God in our resting
Bless the time we lie in bed.

Be thou our vision, Lord
this and every day,
the center of our lives
and the focus of our thoughts.

Be thou our wisdom, Lord
this and every day,

the author of our words
and the impulse of our hearts.

Psalm 23:1-4

(As you read and listen, use the pauses to let the words speak to your hearts)

The Lord is my shepherd, I lack nothing.
He makes me lie down in green pastures

He leads me beside quiet waters,
he refreshes my soul.
He guides me along the right paths
for his name's sake.

(PAUSE)

*Even though I walk
through the darkest valley,
I will fear no evil,
for you are with me;
your rod and your staff,
they comfort me.

The Lord is my shepherd, I lack nothing.
He makes me lie down in green pastures.

**Glory to the Father,
and to the Son,
and to the Holy Spirit,
Three in One. Amen**

For Truth that speaks to hearts
Lord, show us your mercy

*For grace beyond imagining
Lord, show us your mercy

*For forgiveness from our sin
Lord, show us your mercy

God of mercy,
in you alone is the forgiveness
that we long for,
in you alone is the peace
that calms our soul.
Forgive the incompleteness of our faith
and the imperfection in our lives.

God of mercy,
bless these hearts anew,
that we might reveal
the breadth of your grace
and the glory of your love,
through the service of these lives.

If we, in humility, will confess our sins
in the quietness of our hearts or in the company of the
faithful, God's love and mercy bring forgiveness.

Let us share the peace of Christ Jesus with those around us.

'Peace I leave with you,' said Jesus. 'My peace I give you.'
'Again Jesus said, "Peace be with you!"'

(Pause while the peace is shared)

Give thanks to the Lord, for he is good;
His love endures forever

Matthew 6:9-13

> **Our Father in heaven,
> hallowed be your name,**

your kingdom come,
your will be done,
on earth as it is in heaven.
Give us today our daily bread.
And forgive us our debts,
as we also have forgiven our debtors.
And lead us not into temptation,
 but deliver us from the evil one.
Amen

1 Kings 19 (part of vs. 9-13)

And the word of the Lord came to him: "What are you doing here, Elijah? ...Go out and stand on the mountain... for the Lord is about to pass by."

Then a great and powerful wind tore the mountains apart ... but the Lord was not in the wind. After the wind there was an earthquake, but the Lord was not in the earthquake.

(PAUSE)

After the earthquake came a fire, but the Lord was not in the fire. And after the fire came a gentle whisper. When Elijah heard it, he pulled his cloak over his face and went out and stood at the mouth of the cave.

(PAUSE)

In our journeying with you
be our guide, O Lord, we pray.
Open our ears
to the unexpected,
to the gentle whisper
that follows earthquake and fire.
In our journeying with you
open our eyes
to the destination,
and the greener pasture

that you have prepared for us.
In our journeying with you,
be our guide, O Lord, we pray. **Amen.**

God who loves us
Blesséd be your name

God who calls us
Blesséd be your name

God who leads us
Blesséd be your name

God who sends us
Blesséd be your name

Now may the God who leads us
from darkness to light
illuminate our footsteps,
lengthen our stride
and strengthen our resolve,
that we might walk the path
prepared for us,
and faithfully serve our Lord and King.
Amen.

Thursday Midday – Lectio Divina

(Individual or small group)

This is slight variation on an ancient technique of contemplative prayer, which helps us to connect our hearts with the Word of God. It has been kept alive particularly within the Benedictine monastic tradition. It requires that we allow for quietness in the bustle of the day, to listen for the 'gentle whisper' of God. These studies use the Psalms, but any suitable passage (preferably not too long) may be used.

Lectio - Reading

Read twice, slowly and attentively, listening for that 'gentle whisper' that is God's word or phrase for today, using this or an alternative reading.

> 'I sought the Lord, and he answered me;
>   he delivered me from all my fears.
> Those who look to him are radiant;
>   their faces are never covered with shame.
> This poor man called, and the Lord heard him;
>   he saved him out of all his troubles...
> Taste and see that the Lord is good;
>   blessed is the one who takes refuge in him.
> Fear the Lord, you his holy people,
>   for those who fear him lack nothing.
> The lions may grow weak and hungry,
>   but those who seek the Lord lack no good thing.'
> *(Psalm 34:4-6, 8-10)*

Meditatio – Meditation (2-3 min)

As Mary 'pondered in her heart' what she heard and saw of Jesus, so we repeat these words silently and let them sink into our hearts, interact with our day, our thoughts and concerns… God's word becomes our word for today.

(Group – allow time for those who wish to share the word, image or phrase that has touched their heart.)

Oratio - Prayer

As we turn to prayer, so God invites us to respond to the word or phrase that has spoken to us. In the quietness or aloud we bring to Him those words, images or people that God has placed on our hearts, and how we might put those words into action.

(Group – allow time to pray for the person on your right.)

Contemplatio – Contemplation

We spend a minute or two in silence, enjoying the experience of God's presence and love embracing us

> **Glory to the Father,**
> **and to the Son,**
> **and to the Holy Spirit,**
> **Three in One. Amen.**

Thursday Evening

(* Indicates optional change of reader. Bold text to be read by all)

We meet in the unity
of Father, Son
and Holy Spirit,
glorious Trinity.

To the One here with us in our meeting
We lift our hearts in praise

To the One whose love is all-embracing
We lift our hearts in praise

To the One whose grace is so amazing
We lift our hearts in praise

To the One who guides our daily traveling
We lift our hearts in praise

Psalm 36:5-9

(As you read and listen, use the pauses to let the words speak to your hearts)

Your love, Lord, reaches to the heavens,
your faithfulness to the skies.

Your righteousness is like the highest mountains,
your justice like the great deep.
You, Lord, preserve both people and animals.
How priceless is your unfailing love, O God!

(PAUSE)

People take refuge in the shadow of your wings.
They feast on the abundance of your house;
you give them drink from your river of delights.
For with you is the fountain of life;
in your light we see light.

(PAUSE)

Your love, Lord, reaches to the heavens,
your faithfulness to the skies.

**Glory to the Father,
and to the Son,
and to the Holy Spirit,
Three in One. Amen**

Acts 17:25-27

And (God) is not served by human hands, as if he needed anything.
Rather, he himself gives everyone life and breath and everything
else. From one man he made all the nations, that they should
inhabit the whole earth; and he marked out their appointed times in
history and the boundaries of their lands. God did this so that they
would seek him and perhaps reach out for him and find him,
though he is not far from any one of us.

(PAUSE)

Mark 6:39-44

Then Jesus told them to make all the people sit down in groups on
the green grass. So they sat down in groups of hundreds and
fifties. Taking the five loaves and the two fish and looking up to
heaven, he gave thanks and broke the loaves. Then he gave them to
his disciples to distribute to the people. He also divided the two
fish among them all. They all ate and were satisfied, and the
disciples picked up twelve basket-full of broken pieces of bread

and fish. The number of the men who had eaten was five thousand.

(PAUSE)

God who brings us from desolate places
and into his presence.
Accept the gratitude of these hearts.

*God who lifts us from despairing places
and grants to us release.
Accept the gratitude of these hearts.

*God who leads us to sacred places
where we can rest in peace.
Accept the gratitude of these hearts.

Matthew 6:9-13

Our Father in heaven,
hallowed be your name,
your kingdom come,
your will be done,
on earth as it is in heaven.
Give us today our daily bread.
And forgive us our debts,
as we also have forgiven our debtors.
And lead us not into temptation,
but deliver us from the evil one.
Amen

For all who have been led into exile
Lord, have mercy

For all who have been led into slavery
Lord, have mercy

For all who have been led into poverty
Lord, have mercy

For all who have been led into conflict
Lord, have mercy

For all who have been prevented from being
the people they were created to be.
Lord, have mercy

You have fed us with your word,
embraced us with your love
and brought us safely
to the end of this, your day.
For the opportunities
that tomorrow will bring,
walk closely with us, we pray.

May your gentle whisper
be the word we follow,
your hand be the hand we hold
and your footsteps be the marks
in which we place our feet.
Amen.

Friday Morning – The resurrection life

(* Indicates optional change of reader. Bold text to be read by all)

In the name of the loving Father
we greet each other.

In the name of the risen Son
we serve each other.

In the name of the divine Spirit
we bless each other.

In the name of the Three in One
we are united together.

Gracious God,
who brought us out of darkness
into this sacred place,
and through sacrifice
has shown to us such grace.
To you belongs our praise.

*Gracious God,
whose love is beyond imagining,
whose grace extends to all,
accept the praises of your people
wherever they might be,
as joined in spirit
with angels above
we share their glorious song.

**Holy, holy, holy
is the Lord God Almighty,
who was, and is, and is to come!**

To him who sits on the throne and to the Lamb
be praise and honor and glory and power,
for ever and ever,
Amen.

Psalm 107:1-9

(As you read and listen, use the pauses to let the words speak to your hearts)

Give thanks to the Lord, for he is good;
his love endures for ever.

Let the redeemed of the Lord tell their story –
those he redeemed from the hand of the foe,
those he gathered from the lands,
from east and west, from north and south.
Some wandered in desert wastelands,
finding no way to a city where they could settle.
They were hungry and thirsty, and their lives ebbed away.
Then they cried out to the Lord in their trouble,
and he delivered them from their distress.

(PAUSE)

*He led them by a straight way
to a city where they could settle.
Let them give thanks to the Lord for his unfailing love
and his wonderful deeds for mankind,
for he satisfies the thirsty and fills the hungry with good
things.

Give thanks to the Lord, for he is good;
his love endures for ever.

**Glory to the Father,
and to the Son,
and to the Holy Spirit,
Three in One. Amen**

For all we have said or done
that has proved unfruitful
and caused you pain,
God of mercy,
Forgive us.

*For all we have left undone
that would have blessed someone
who was in need,
God of mercy,
Forgive us.

Be assured, our God is merciful and forgives those
who humbly turn to him in repentance.
Give thanks to the Lord, for he is good
His love endures forever

Isaiah 35:1,2,5,6

The desert and the parched land will be glad;
the wilderness will rejoice and blossom.
Like the crocus, it will burst into bloom;
it will rejoice greatly and shout for joy.
The glory of Lebanon will be given to it,
the splendor of Carmel and Sharon;
they will see the glory of the Lord,
the splendor of our God.

(PAUSE)

*Then will the eyes of the blind be opened
and the ears of the deaf unstopped.

Then will the lame leap like a deer,
and the mute tongue shout for joy.
Water will gush forth in the wilderness
and streams in the desert.

(PAUSE)

Matthew 6:9-13

Our Father in heaven,
hallowed be your name,
your kingdom come,
your will be done,
on earth as it is in heaven.
Give us today our daily bread.
And forgive us our debts,
as we also have forgiven our debtors.
And lead us not into temptation,
but deliver us from the evil one.
Amen

It is a wonderful truth
that you have already walked
the path that we now follow
known hardship, temptation and suffering
and yet grace love to all.
And with that knowledge deep in our hearts
we can follow you in confidence,
and when difficulties arise
listen for your footfall.

Let it be known
throughout the world
We serve a risen Lord.

*Let it be seen
throughout the world
We serve a risen Lord.

*Let it be felt
throughout the world
We serve a risen Lord.

In the words that we shall speak
may the Spirit of Truth be with us.
In the actions of our hands
may the Spirit of Love be with us.
In the places we shall go
may the Spirit of Peace be with us.

Friday Midday - Lectio Divina

(Individual or small group)

This is slight variation on an ancient technique of contemplative prayer, which helps us to connect our hearts with the Word of God. It has been kept alive particularly within the Benedictine monastic tradition. It requires that we allow for quietness in the bustle of the day, to listen for the 'gentle whisper' of God. These studies use the Psalms, but any suitable passage (preferably not too long) may be used.

Lectio - Reading

Read twice, slowly and attentively, listening for that 'gentle whisper' that is God's word or phrase for today, using this or an alternative reading.

> Your love, Lord, reaches to the heavens,
> your faithfulness to the skies.
> Your righteousness is like the highest mountains,
> your justice like the great deep.
> You, Lord, preserve both people and animals.
> How priceless is your unfailing love, O God!
> People take refuge in the shadow of your wings.
> They feast in the abundance of your house;
> you give them drink from your river of delights.
> For with you is the fountain of life;
> in your light we see light.
> *(Psalm 36:5-9)*

Meditatio – Meditation (2-3 min)

As Mary 'pondered in her heart' what she heard and saw of Jesus, so we repeat these words silently and let them sink into our hearts, interact with our day, our thoughts and concerns… God's word becomes our word for today.

(Group – allow time for those who wish to share the word, image or phrase that has touched their heart.)

Oratio - Prayer

As we turn to prayer, so God invites us to respond to the word or phrase that has spoken to us. In the quietness or aloud we bring to Him those words, images or people that God has placed on our hearts, and how we might put those words into action.

(Group – allow time to pray for the person on your right.)

Contemplatio – Contemplation

We spend a minute or two in silence, enjoying the experience of God's presence and love embracing us

**Glory to the Father,
and to the Son,
and to the Holy Spirit,
Three in One. Amen**

Friday Evening

(* Indicates optional change of reader. Bold text to be read by all)

God is with us as we meet,
his voice discerned
through Scripture's Word
and in our prayer.
God is with us as we meet,
his presence felt
as hearts are warmed
and love is shared.
God is with us as we meet

Lord, open these eyes
That we might see this world's beauty.

Lord, open these ears
That we might discern your calling.

Lord, open these hearts
That we might be led to service.

Lord, open these mouths
That we might proclaim your Word.

Psalm 121

(As you read and listen, use the pauses to let the words speak to your hearts)

I lift up my eyes to the mountains –
where does my help come from?
My help comes from the Lord,
the Maker of heaven and earth.

*He will not let your foot slip –
he who watches over you will not slumber;
indeed, he who watches over Israel
will neither slumber nor sleep.

(PAUSE)

*The Lord watches over you –
the Lord is your shade at your right hand;
the sun will not harm you by day,
nor the moon by night.

(PAUSE)

*The Lord will keep you from all harm –
he will watch over your life;
the Lord will watch over your coming and going
both now and for evermore.

I lift up my eyes to the mountains –
where does my help come from?
**My help comes from the Lord,
the Maker of heaven and earth.**

**Glory to the Father,
and to the Son,
and to the Holy Spirit,
Three in One. Amen**

1 Corinthians 1:26,27

Brothers and sisters, think of what you were when you were called.
Not many of you were wise by human standards; not many were
influential; not many were of noble birth. But God chose the
foolish things of the world to shame the wise; God chose the weak
things of the world to shame the strong.

(PAUSE)

John 13:12-17

When he had finished washing their feet, he put on his clothes and returned to his place. 'Do you understand what I have done for you?' he asked them. 'You call me "Teacher" and "Lord", and rightly so, for that is what I am. Now that I, your Lord and Teacher, have washed your feet, you also should wash one another's feet. I have set you an example that you should do as I have done for you.'

(PAUSE)

Gracious God
who fills our lives with love
Be the love that dwells between us.

Gracious God
who fills our lives with peace
Be the peace that dwells between us.

Gracious God
who fills our lives with joy
Be the joy that dwells between us

Matthew 6:9-13

**Our Father in heaven,
hallowed be your name,
your kingdom come,
your will be done,
on earth as it is in heaven.
Give us today our daily bread.
And forgive us our debts,
as we also have forgiven our debtors.
And lead us not into temptation,
but deliver us from the evil one.
Amen**

For a world that lives
but has yet to experience life in all its fullness.
Precious Lord, have mercy.

For a world that loves,
but has yet to meet with the source of all love.
Precious Lord, have mercy.

For a world that seeks,
but forever stumbles in its searching.
Precious Lord, have mercy.

May God's love be the love
that surrounds us today.
May God's peace be the peace
that we share on our way.
May God's grace be the grace
that our actions display.
May God's truth be the truth
in the words that we say.

Saturday Morning - The call to follow

(* Indicates optional change of reader. Bold text to be read by all)

The God who calls us
is with us as we meet.
The God who guides us
reveals to us the route.
The God who feeds us
supplies us with his truth.
The God who loves us
inspires us as we speak.

For the world in which we walk,
Creator God, we give our thanks.

For footsteps to follow,
Living God, we give our thanks.

For people encountered,
Loving God, we give our thanks.

For blessings offered,
Caring God, we give our thanks.

For blessings received,
Gracious God, we give our thanks.

For the world in which we walk,
Creator God, we give our thanks.

Psalm 34:1-10

(As you read and listen, use the pauses to let the words speak to your hearts)

I will extol the Lord at all times;
his praise will always be on my lips.

I will glory in the Lord;
let the afflicted hear and rejoice.
Glorify the Lord with me:
let us exalt his name together.
I sought the Lord, and he answered me;
he delivered me from all my fears.

(PAUSE)

*Those who look to him are radiant;
their faces are never covered with shame.
This poor man called, and the Lord heard him;
he saved him out of all his troubles.
The angel of the Lord encamps around those who fear him,
and he delivers them.

(PAUSE)

*Taste and see that the Lord is good;
blessed is the one who takes refuge in him.
Fear the Lord, you his holy people,
for those who fear him lack nothing.
The lions may grow weak and hungry,
 but those who seek the Lord lack no good thing.
I will extol the Lord at all times;
his praise will always be on my lips.

Glory to the Father,
and to the Son,
and to the Holy Spirit,
Three in One. Amen

Lead us to a mountaintop
within our daily lives,
a sacred space
where life takes on
a different pace,
for we are too busy, Lord,
and fail to hear your call.

*Lead us to a mountaintop
within our daily lives,
a quiet place
where we can rest
in your embrace,
for we are too busy, Lord,
and fail to hear your call.

If we, in humility, will confess our sins
in the quietness of our hearts or in the company of the
faithful, God's love and mercy bring forgiveness.

Let us share the peace of Christ Jesus with those around us.

'Peace I leave with you,' said Jesus. 'My peace I give you.'
'Again Jesus said, "Peace be with you!"'

(Pause while the peace is shared)

Give thanks to the Lord, for he is good;
His love endures forever

Matthew 6:9-13

Our Father in heaven,
hallowed be your name,
your kingdom come,
your will be done,
on earth as it is in heaven.
Give us today our daily bread.
And forgive us our debts,
as we also have forgiven our debtors.

And lead us not into temptation,
but deliver us from the evil one.
Amen

1 Samuel 3:8-10

A third time the Lord called, 'Samuel!' And Samuel got up and
went to Eli and said, 'Here I am; you called me.'
Then Eli realized that the Lord was calling the boy. So Eli told
Samuel, 'Go and lie down, and if he calls you, say, "Speak, Lord,
for your servant is listening."' So Samuel went and lay down in his
place.
The Lord came and stood there, calling as at the other times,
'Samuel! Samuel!'
Then Samuel said, 'Speak, for your servant is listening.'

(PAUSE)

Send us out into the world, Lord
To speak your words of truth

Send us out into the world, Lord
To proclaim your love and grace

Send us out into the world, Lord
To bring comfort to the weak

Send us out into the world, Lord
To be your hands and feet.

We shall not fear this day
for you are with us
wherever we might go,
your light to shine ahead,
your footsteps to lead the way.

We shall not fear this day
for your word will be our guide,

your strength sustain us,
and your love revive us
this day and all days.

We shall not fear this day
for you are with us
wherever we might go.

So may the God we follow
be the voice that calls us,
the feet that guide us,
the love that inspires us,
the strength that sustains us
and the embrace
that welcome us home.

Saturday Midday - Lectio Divina

(Individual or small group)

This is slight variation on an ancient technique of contemplative prayer, which helps us to connect our hearts with the Word of God. It has been kept alive particularly within the Benedictine monastic tradition. It requires that we allow for quietness in the bustle of the day, to listen for the 'gentle whisper' of God. These studies use the Psalms, but any suitable passage (preferably not too long) may be used.

Lectio - Reading

Read twice, slowly and attentively, listening for that 'gentle whisper' that is God's word or phrase for today, using this or an alternative reading.

> How good and pleasant it is
> when God's people live together in unity!
> It is like precious oil poured on the head,
> running down on the beard,
> running down on Aaron's beard,
> down on the collar of his robe.
> It is as if the dew of Hermon
> were falling on Mount Zion.
> For there the Lord bestows his blessing,
> even life for evermore.
> (Psalm 133)

Meditatio – Meditation (2-3 min)

As Mary 'pondered in her heart' what she heard and saw of Jesus, so we repeat these words silently and let them sink into our hearts, interact with our day, our thoughts and concerns... God's word becomes our word for today.

(Group – allow time for those who wish to share the word, image or phrase that has touched their heart.)

Oratio - Prayer

As we turn to prayer, so God invites us to respond to the word or phrase that has spoken to us. In the quietness or aloud we bring to Him those words, images or people that God has placed on our hearts, and how we might put those words into action.

(Group – allow time to pray for the person on your right.)

Contemplatio – Contemplation

We spend a minute or two in silence, enjoying the experience of God's presence and love embracing us

**Glory to the Father,
and to the Son,
and to the Holy Spirit,
Three in One. Amen.**

Saturday Evening

(* Indicates optional change of reader. Bold text to be read by all)

We meet together
in the name of God the Father,
God the Son
and God the Holy Spirit,
our lives united
in the Three in One.

For your love which breathed this world into being,
and daily sustains it
We give you thanks

For your love which granted mankind
free will and choice
We give you thanks

For your love which never fails as we do,
but stretches to eternity
We give you thanks

For your love which rose triumphant from the grave
and lives within us
We give you thanks

For your love which encircles us as we meet
together in your presence
We give you thanks

Psalm 46:1-3, 8-10

(As you read and listen, use the pauses to let the words speak to your hearts)

God is our refuge and strength,
an ever-present help in trouble.

Therefore we will not fear, though the earth give way
and the mountains fall into the heart of the sea,
though its waters roar and foam
and the mountains quake with their surging.

(PAUSE)

Come and see what the Lord has done,
the desolations he has brought on the earth.
He makes wars cease
to the ends of the earth.
He breaks the bow and shatters the spear;
he burns the shields with fire.
He says, 'Be still, and know that I am God;
I will be exalted among the nations,
I will be exalted in the earth.'

God is our refuge and strength,
an ever-present help in trouble.

Glory to the Father,
and to the Son,
and to the Holy Spirit,
Three in One. Amen

Luke 2:28-32

Simeon took (Jesus) in his arms and praised God, saying:

'Sovereign Lord, as you have promised you may now dismiss your servant in peace. For my eyes have seen your salvation, which you have prepared in the sight of all nations: a light for revelation to the Gentiles, and the glory of your people Israel

(PAUSE)

Hebrews 8:10

This is the covenant I will establish with the people of Israel after that time, declares the Lord. I will put my laws in their minds and write them on their hearts. I will be their God, and they will be my people.

(PAUSE)

Fill us with your Spirit
That our faith might be enriched

Fill us with your Spirit
That our lives might be empowered

Fill us with your Spirit
That our witness might be emboldened

Fill us with your Spirit
That your name might be glorified

Matthew 6:9-13

Our Father in heaven,
hallowed be your name,
your kingdom come,
your will be done,
on earth as it is in heaven.
Give us today our daily bread.
And forgive us our debts,
as we also have forgiven our debtors.
And lead us not into temptation,
but deliver us from the evil one.

Wherever your love pours out from hearts
God of love, may lives be blessed.

Wherever your hands are seen in ours
Servant God, may lives be blessed.

Wherever your peace is sown like seeds
God of peace, may lives be blessed.

Wherever your grace sets prisoners free
God of grace, may lives be blessed.

Wherever your joy shines out in praise
God of joy, may lives be blessed.

Now may the grace of God,
Father, Son and Spirit,
uphold us through this night,
and bring us refreshed
to the joys and challenge
of another day.
Amen

9 Traditional Celtic Festivals

Is it a good thing for Christians to be looking at these more natural festivals and even celebrating them?

Well, I think if you strip them down to their bare essentials then there is something to be learned and celebrated in these seasonal festivals. Christianity tried to blot them out and replace them, but maybe we should have looked more closely at the social and cultural reasons behind them, and brought our Christian perspective and knowledge of God into them.

Samhain (1st November)

The festival of Samhain (pronounced 'sow'inn' and the word for November in some Gaelic languages) is a celebration of the end of the harvest season in Gaelic culture, and is sometimes regarded as the Celtic New Year.

Samhain has been celebrated in Britain for centuries and has its origin in Pagan Celtic traditions. It was the time of year when the veils between this world and the Otherworld were believed to be at their thinnest: when the spirits of the dead could most readily mingle again with the living. Later, when the festival was adopted by Christians, it was celebrated as All Hallows' Eve, followed by All Saints Day, though it still retained elements of remembering and honoring the dead.

A visual aid - an apple - might be placed centrally to the gathered group. The apple tree had significance to the pagan Celts which we can also appreciate at this time. It comes into blossom in the spring (the Celts saw this as a symbol of love and fertility) and throughout the year the fruit continues to develop and ripen. Because many varieties keep over a long period of time when stored this was symbolic of love's presence, even long past the time of peak ripeness. The apple, of course, should it fall to the ground contains the seeds from which life begins again.

Imbolc - 1st or 2nd February

Imbolc most commonly is celebrated on February 1st or 2nd, since this is the cross-quarter day on the solar calendar, halfway between the Winter Solstice and the Spring Equinox in the northern hemisphere. Among agrarian peoples, Imbolc has been traditionally associated with the onset of lactation of ewes, soon to give birth to the spring lambs. The holiday was a festival of the hearth and home, and a celebration of the lengthening days.

The Christian Church sought to introduce an alternative festival with the Feast of the Presentation of Jesus at the Temple, also known as Candlemas (when all the Church's candles were blessed) or the Feast of the Purification of the Virgin, which falls on or around 1 February .

The feast day of Saint Brighid falls on 1 February, in Ireland. There, some of the old customs have survived. On Imbolc Eve, Brighid was said to visit virtuous households and bless the inhabitants as they slept. As Brighid represented the light half of the year, and the power that will bring people from the dark season of winter into spring, her presence was very important at this time of year.

Brighid's crosses (pictured left) were made at Imbolc. A Brighid's cross consists of rushes woven into a shape similar to a swastika, with a square in the middle and four arms protruding from each corner. They were often hung over doors, windows and stables to welcome Brighid and protect the buildings from fire and lightning.

Beltane - 1st May

Beltane (Old Irish Bealtaine – pronounced Bee-Al-tin-aye) is mentioned in some of the earliest Irish literature and it is associated with important events in Irish mythology. It marked the beginning of the pastoral summer season when the herds of livestock were driven out to the summer pastures and mountain grazing lands. Rituals were performed to protect the cattle, crops and people, and to encourage growth. Most commonly it is held on 30 April - 1 May, or halfway between the spring equinox and the summer solstice

Special bonfires were kindled, and their flames, smoke and ashes were deemed to have protective powers. The people and their cattle would walk around the bonfire, or between two bonfires, and sometimes leap over flames or embers. All household fires would be doused and then re-lit from the Beltane bonfire.

Another common aspect of the festival which survived up until the early 20th century in Ireland was the hanging of May Boughs on the doors and windows of houses and the erection of May Bushes in farmyards.

Lughnasadh - 1st August

Lughnasadh (pronounced Loo-nuh-sa) marked the beginning of the harvest season, the ripening of first fruits, and was traditionally a time of community gatherings, market festivals, horse races and reunions with distant family and friends.

On mainland Europe and in Ireland many people continue to celebrate the holiday with bonfires and dancing.

The Christian church has established the ritual of blessing the fields on this day and in some English-speaking countries in the Northern Hemisphere the first day of August is Lammas Day (loaf-mass day), the festival of the first wheat harvest of the year. On this day it was customary to bring to church a loaf made from the new crop.

In many parts of England, tenants were bound to present freshly harvested wheat to their landlords on or before the first day of August. In the Anglo-Saxon Chronicle, where it is referred to regularly, it is called "the feast of first fruits". The blessing of new fruits was performed annually in both the Eastern and Western Churches on the first, or the sixth, of August.

Lughnasadh customs persisted widely until the 20th century, with the event being variously named 'Garland Sunday', 'Bilberry Sunday', 'Mountain Sunday' and 'Crom Dubh Sunday'. The custom of climbing hills and mountains at Lughnasadh has survived in some areas, although it has been re-cast as a Christian pilgrimage.

Winter Solstice -22nd December

Though the winter solstice lasts only an instant in time, the term is also colloquially used as midwinter or contrastingly the first day of winter, to refer to the day on which it occurs. More evident to those in high latitudes, this occurs on the shortest day, and longest night, and the sun's daily maximum position in the sky is the lowest.

The seasonal significance of the winter solstice is in the reversal of the gradual lengthening of nights and shortening of days. Depending on the shift of the Gregorian calendar, the winter solstice occurs on December 21 or 22 each year in the Northern Hemisphere, and June 20 or 21 in the Southern Hemisphere.

In prehistoric times, winter was a very difficult time for people in the northern latitudes. The growing season had ended and the tribe had to live off stored food and whatever animals they could catch. The people would be troubled as the life-giving sun sank lower in the sky each noon. They feared that it would eventually disappear and leave them in permanent darkness and extreme cold. After the winter solstice, they would have reason to celebrate as they saw the sun rising and strengthening once more.

Although many months of cold weather remained before spring, they took heart that the return of the warm season was inevitable. The concept of birth and or death/rebirth became associated with the winter solstice.

(Source, www.religioustolerance.org/winter_solstice.htm)

A Liturgy for Samhain

Let's just spend a moment or two in quietness.

The day is yours, and yours also the night; you established the sun and moon. It was you who set all the boundaries of the earth; you made both summer and winter.   *(Psalm 74:16-17)*

(PAUSE)

*In the fading of the summer sun,
the shortening of days, cooling breeze,
swallows' flight and moonlight rays
We see the Creator's hand

*In the browning of leaves once green,
morning mists, autumn chill,
fruit that falls, frost's first kiss
We see the Creator's hand

Creator God, forgive our moments of ingratitude,
the spiritual blindness that prevents us
from appreciating the wonder that is this world,
the endless cycle of nature,
of life and death and rebirth.
Forgive us for taking without giving,
reaping without sowing.
Open our eyes to see
our lips to praise,

our hands to share,
and may our feet tread lightly
on the road that we must travel.

(Here a song, chant or hymn might be sung)

By faith
we gaze up to the heavens
and know
within its vastness
that this is your creation,
planned and effected within eternity

*By faith
we pluck an ear of corn
and know
within its symmetry
lies the chemistry of life,
the potential of creation within our hand.

*By faith
we listen for your voice
and know
the whisper that we hear
breathed a world into existence
yet listens to a prayer within our heart.

*By faith
we strive to do your will
and know
the door that we approach
may lead us to shadows,
where our role is to become your light.

*By faith
we cling to your word
and know
the strength that we receive
has its source within the love
that is at the center of all things.

For summer's passing
and harvest home
We thank you

*For autumn's splendor
and winter's chill
We thank you

*For seed that has fallen,
the promise of spring
We thank you

St. Francis of Assisi wrote these wise words:

"Remember that when you leave this earth,
you can take nothing that you have received
…but only what you have given"

Psalm 92:12-14

*The righteous will flourish like a palm tree,
they will grow like a cedar of Lebanon;
planted in the house of the Lord,
they will flourish in the courts of our God.
They will still bear fruit in old age,
they will stay fresh and green.

**Glory to the Father,
and to the Son,
and to the Holy Spirit,
Three in One. Amen**

For fruitfulness
We thank you

For a generous spirit
We thank you

For wisdom and faith
We thank you

For old age and new birth
We thank you

For those who have gone before us,
seeds planted in your rich pasture
with the hope of life eternal,
may their enduring spirit live on,
enriching and empowering our lives,
their love linger,
their presence be near
until we meet once more.

*For your embracing love;
a Father's love,
a Mother's love,
a love that sees our failings
and forgives us.
A love that sees our joys
and embraces us.
A love that knows no end
or beginning.
A love that could die for us.
We bless you.
We bless you

(Here a song, chant or hymn might be sung)

Together we say:

We bless you
God of seed time and harvest,
and we bless each other,
that the beauty of this world,
and the love that created it,
might be expressed though our lives
and be a blessing to others,
now and always. Amen.

A Liturgy for Imbolc

(* Indicates optional change of reader. Bold text to be read by all)

Springtime!
The promise of new life

*Springtime!
The potential for growth

*Springtime!
The hope of harvests to come

Jeremiah 5:24

Let us fear the Lord our God,
who gives autumn and spring rains in season,
who assures us of the regular weeks of harvest.

In the lengthening of days,
new life emerging
from winter's frozen ground
We see the Creator's hand

*In the sight of a tiny lamb,
joyfully bounding
across hillside farm
We see the Creator's hand

Creator God,
you gifted this world
and made us stewards of it,
gave us family from many lands
and ask us to care for them,
put your word upon our heart
and ask that we share it.
But we have thought only of ourselves
and the blessings of our lives,
forgetting that your grace
and love are for the benefit of all.
Forgive our selfishness,
enlarge our vision,
and enable us to become
the people we could be,
faithful servants
of our heavenly King

(Here a song, chant or hymn might be sung)

Psalm 8

Lord, our Lord,
how majestic is your name in all the earth!

You have set your glory in the heavens.
Through the praise of children and infants
you have established a stronghold against your enemies,
to silence the foe and the avenger.

(PAUSE)

*When I consider your heavens, the work of your fingers,
the moon and the stars, which you have set in place,
what is mankind that you are mindful of them,
human beings that you care for them?

(PAUSE)

*You have made them a little lower than the angels
and crowned them with glory and honor.
You made them rulers over the works of your hands;
you put everything under their feet: all flocks and herds,
and the animals of the wild, the birds in the sky,
and the fish in the sea, all that swim the paths of the seas.

Lord, our Lord,
how majestic is your name in all the earth!

Glory to the Father,
and to the Son,
and to the Holy Spirit,
Three in One. Amen

A sleeping world emerges to new possibilities,
weakening winter's icy grip,
and birdsong and bleating lamb
announce to all the promise
that in due season
creation bursts into life.
Leaves that fell in autumn
lie upon the ground
soon to feed the earth,
and in nature's wondrous cycle
of death and rebirth
within the tree is a stirring of new growth

For the cycle of life
which brings death and rebirth
We rejoice in the promise of spring

*For lengthening days
and sunlight's warmth upon the soil
We rejoice in the promise of spring

*For a snowdrop's beauty
reflecting its Creator's artistry
We rejoice in the promise of spring

*For new born lambs,
their joy and exuberance
We rejoice in the promise of spring

For all of creation
and the majesty of its Creator
We rejoice in the promise of spring

This is your garden, Creator God,
a thing of beauty
beyond understanding,
a poem that is being written
not in words
but in colors,
wind's whisper,
soaring bird,
snowdrop's petal,
gentle rain,
sunlight's warmth.
This is your garden, Creator God,
a thing of beauty
beyond understanding,
gifted to us in love.

(A time of intercession might be appropriate at this point, either
silent or aloud, praying for areas of the world where humankind is
not in harmony with creation, pollution threatens health and
livelihoods, rain forests are being decimated, and where there is
hunger or poverty)

(PAUSE)

Together we say
We bless you
God of seed time and harvest,
and we bless each other,

that the beauty of this world,
and the love that created it,
might be expressed though our lives
and be a blessing to others,
now and always
Amen.

.

A Liturgy for Beltane

(* Indicates optional change of reader. Bold text to be read by all)

Let's just spend a moment or two in quietness. Consider winter's chill when all was still, with seed and plant lying dormant. Then the rising sun and warming air of spring, green shoots emerging, leaves unfurling, blossom displaying its praise to the Creator.

(PAUSE)

God of winter's cold, of clear sky, frozen rivers
We praise your Holy Name

God of spring's warmth, April showers, waking life
We praise your Holy Name

God of summer sun, warming earth, sprouting seed
We praise your Holy Name

God of summer pasture and mountain stream
We praise your Holy Name

God of root and shoot, of harvest to come
We praise your Holy Name

We are drawn to your feet in worship,
your creation facing its creator,

95

hearts laid bare by your light,
humbly asking for your mercy.
We come to you as a people in need
of assurance and forgiveness.
We come to you as a people in need
of healing and wholeness.
We come dependent upon your love.
Draw us close.
Enfold us in your arms.
Fill us with your Spirit
that we might reflect your light
within this dark world,
speak your Word with boldness
and draw others to your feet.
We ask this through your dear Son Jesus Christ.
Amen

(Here a song, chant or hymn might be sung)

The warmth of the sun's embrace,
the gentle breeze swept in by incoming tide,
the rhythm of seasons,
of new birth,
death and recreation.
All these speak so clearly of your love,
your power,
and your beauty.
All are expressions of your creativity
and more importantly of yourself.
As an artist might share his personality
within each brush-stroke,
so within the myriad colors of a butterfly's wing
you share the exuberance of your love.
That we can glimpse you within creation
is a beautiful thought,
but also tells us that you desire to be seen,
to be found and known.
Open our eyes, Lord,

as we walk through this world,
feel the wind and sunshine,
see the majesty of creation unfolding before our eyes.
Help us to see you.

Psalm 65:9-13

The whole earth is filled with awe at your wonders;
where morning dawns, where evening fades,
you call forth songs of joy.

*You care for the land and water it;
you enrich it abundantly.
The streams of God are filled with water
to provide the people with corn,
for so you have ordained it.

*You drench its furrows and level its ridges;
you soften it with showers and bless its crops.
You crown the year with your bounty,
and your carts overflow with abundance.

*The grasslands of the wilderness overflow;
the hills are clothed with gladness.
The meadows are covered with flocks
and the valleys are mantled with corn;
they shout for joy and sing.

The whole earth is filled with awe at your wonders;
where morning dawns, where evening fades,
you call forth songs of joy.

Glory to the Father,
and to the Son,
and to the Holy Spirit,
Three in One. Amen

(A time of intercession might be appropriate at this point, either silent or aloud, praying for areas of the world where life is a struggle. For those whose lives lack hope, who cannot see the beauty in the world because they live in poverty, who fear for another failed harvest and hunger to follow)

(PAUSE)

God of renewal,
of life and death,
rebirth
Renew our hearts and minds

*God of promise,
of all beginnings,
and endings
Renew our hearts and minds

*God of hope,
of new growth,
and harvest
Renew our hearts and minds

Together we say:

**We bless you
God of seed time and harvest,
and we bless each other,
that the beauty of this world,
and the love that created it,
might be expressed though our lives
and be a blessing to others,
now and always
Amen.**

A Liturgy for Lughnasadh

(* Indicates optional change of reader. Bold text to be read by all)

The earth is the Lord's
And all that is upon it
Created and creative things
Fruit and fruitfulness
Springtime and Summer
Seed-time and harvest

For the promise of harvest
contained within a seed
we thank you.

For the oak tree
within an acorn,
the bread
within a grain,
the apple
within a pip.
The mystery of nature
gift wrapped
for us to sow,
we thank you.

Gen 8:22

As long as the earth endures, seed-time and harvest, cold and heat,
summer and winter, day and night will never cease.

(PAUSE)

We see signs of summer's passing in golden leaves,
shortening days, misty mornings, autumn glow.
We sense its passing in rain that dampens,
winds that chill, Harvest's bounty placed on show.
Creator God, who brings forth
both green shoot and hoar frost,
sunrise and sunset,
we bring our thanks
for seeds that have grown,
harvests gathered,
storehouses filled,
mouths fed.
And, as your good earth rests
through winter's cold embrace,
we look forward to its re-awakening
when kissed by spring's first touch.

Psalm 67

May the peoples praise you, God;
may all the peoples praise you.

May God be gracious to us and bless us
and make his face shine on us
so that your ways may be known on earth,
your salvation among all nations.
May the peoples praise you, God;
may all the peoples praise you.

*May the nations be glad and sing for joy,
for you rule the peoples with equity
and guide the nations of the earth.
May the peoples praise you, God;
may all the peoples praise you.

*The land yields its harvest;
God, our God, blesses us.
May God bless us still,
so that all the ends of the earth will fear him.

May the peoples praise you, God;
may all the peoples praise you.

**Glory to the Father,
and to the Son,
and to the Holy Spirit,
Three in One.** Amen

(Here a song, chant or hymn might be sung)

For creativity in its many forms
we give you thanks.
For the skill of weaver,
potter, artist, sculptor,
needle worker,
all who take that which you have given
and make with it something of beauty.

For fruitfulness in its many forms
we give you thanks.
For selfless love,
grace, wisdom, knowledge,
sacrifice,
all who take that which you have given
and make with it something of beauty

Leviticus 23:16,22

Celebrate the Festival of Harvest with the first-fruits of the crops
you sow in your field. 'Celebrate the Festival of Ingathering at the
end of the year, when you gather in your crops from the field...

(PAUSE)

When you reap the harvest of your land, do not reap to the very
edges of your field or gather the gleanings of your harvest. Leave

them for the poor and for the foreigner residing among you. I am
the Lord your God.

(PAUSE)

(A time of intercession might be appropriate at this point,
either silent or aloud, praying for areas of the world where
harvests are uncertain because of drought or warfare, but
also praying for fruitfulness wherever it might be shown -
lives dedicated to serving others, for artists and craft workers
who take the natural things of this world and make
something beautiful from them)

(PAUSE)

For summer's passing
and harvest home
We thank you

For seed that has fallen
and the promise of spring
We thank you

Together we say:

We bless you
God of seed time and harvest,
and we bless each other,
that the beauty of this world,
and the love that created it,
might be expressed though our lives
and be a blessing to others,
now and always
Amen.

A Liturgy for Winter Solstice

(* Indicates optional change of reader. Bold text to be read by all)

(Place a small table at the center of the group, and upon it place a small candle or tea light for each person present, a few fallen leaves and some seeds)

Seeds sown in spring have grown, fruited and provided for our needs. Trees that provided shelter for wildlife have now shed their leaves, which in due course will decay and provide nutrients for the coming year. Plants in our gardens which are seemingly dead lie dormant within the ground, ready to emerge and bring us joy in the spring to come.

(PAUSE)

Together we say:
You are worthy, our Lord and God,
to receive glory and honor and power,
for you created all things,
and by your will they were created and have their being

This is the God we serve,
a God of love, of healing and power.
Alleluia

This is the God we serve,
a God who loves us with a Father's love.
Alleluia

This is the God we serve,
a God who laughs as we laugh,
Alleluia

This is the God we serve,
a God who suffers as we suffer.
Alleluia

This is the God we serve,
a God who brings light into dark places.
Alleluia

This is the God we serve,
a God who brings warmth into hearts that are chilled.
Alleluia

This is the God we serve,
a God who sees within us the potential of Spring.
Alleluia

(Here a song, chant or hymn might be sung)

There is a winter in all of our lives,
a chill and darkness that makes us yearn
for days that have gone
or put our hope in days yet to be.

*Father God, you created seasons for a purpose.
Spring is full of expectation
buds breaking
frosts abating and an awakening
of creation before the first days of summer.

*Now the sun gives warmth
and comfort to our lives
reviving aching joints
bringing color, new life
and crops to fruiting.

*Autumn gives nature space
to lean back, relax and enjoy the fruits of its labor
mellow colors in sky and landscape
as the earth prepares to rest.

*Then winter, cold and bare as nature takes stock,
rests, unwinds, sleeps until the time is right.
An endless cycle
and yet a perfect model.

*We need a winter in our lives.
A time of rest, a time to stand still.
A time to reacquaint ourselves
with the faith in which we live and breathe.
It is only then that we can draw strength
from the one in whom we are rooted,
take time to grow and rise through the darkness
into the warm glow of your springtime,
to blossom and flourish,
bring color and vitality into this world,
your garden.

**Thank you Father
for the seasons of our lives**

(The candles, if present can be lit at this time)

Let us spend a moment or two looking at these symbols. The
leaves which once were green now withered, fallen to the ground.
They are still a part of God's plan, containing within them food for
new growth. The seed, seemingly without life and yet within it
holding the potential for great beauty or fruitfulness. The flickering
light which illuminates even the darkest of days.

(PAUSE)

With all of our strengths and weaknesses,
hopes and fears,
we come to you now,
our Creator God.
Fill us, renew us,
take us, use us
as your lights in a world of darkness,
empowered through your Spirit,
your Spirit of love,
your Spirit of peace,
your Spirit of hope
in a world that lives but has yet
to experience life in all its fullness,
a world that loves, but has yet
to meet with the source of all love,
a world that forever seeks, but stumbles in its searching.

(Here a song, chant or hymn might be sung)

As we think of those leaves, and the passing of winter
through to the hope of a springtime when life will emerge
from the frozen earth, we remember that we also are a part
of that cycle of death and rebirth, that the seeds we sow in
this life will fall to the ground with the potential to grow and
be fruitful.

As a part of nature's wondrous cycle
of new birth, growth, fruitfulness and death
we rejoice in the creation of new life,
for parenthood, the passing on of knowledge,
understanding and the wisdom of years.
We are grateful for those who have gone before,
passing on to us our spiritual heritage.
May our lives blossom as the apple tree in spring.
May we become fruitful in thought and deed

and may the seed of love that falls to the ground
linger beyond our time upon this earth.

God of winter, springtime
summer and autumn,
God of Light
God of Warmth
God of Love
God of Potential
God of Hope
who in the darkest days
enters our lives
as you entered this world,
bringing love
healing and wholeness
We praise your glorious name!

Together we say:

**We bless you
God of seed time and harvest,
and we bless each other,
that the beauty of this world,
and the love that created it,
might be expressed though our lives
and be a blessing to others,
now and always
Amen.**

Celtic Blessings

God's presence be with you,
Spirit's breath refresh you,
Son's love sustain you
and the power of the Three
be revealed through your life
today and every day.

May the cleansing water
of God's love refresh you,
the gentle breeze
of God's Spirit revive you,
and the radiance
of God's Son surround you,
this day and all days.

Deep in your heart
The Father's grace
The Saviour's love
The Spirit's power
The Three in One
Godhead's unity
Deep in your heart

The embrace of the Father
Be the comfort you desire.
The name of the Son
Be the one on whom you rely.
The presence of the Spirit
Be with you every hour.
The Three in One
Be the focus of all you are.

Bless this house and those within.
Bless our giving and receiving.
Bless our words and conversation.
Bless our hands and recreation.
Bless our sowing and our growing.
Bless our coming and our going.
Bless all who enter and depart.
Bless this house, your peace impart.

May the God of peace
bring peace to this house.
May the Son of peace
bring peace to this house.
May the Spirit of peace
bring peace to this house,
this night and all nights.

References

http://www.valyermo.com/ld-art.html - The author (Fr. Luke Dysinger, O.S.B.) considers this article to be in the Public Domain. This article may therefore be downloaded, reproduced and distributed without special permission from the author. It was first published in the Spring, 1990 (vol.1, no.1) edition of Valyermo Benedictine.

Bradshaw Paul F., Reconstructing Early Christian Worship, SPCK, 2009.

Adam, David, The Rhythm of Life, Triangle, 1996.

Birch, John, Footfall (Prayers for the Journey), Moorleys.

Birch, John, Ripples (Engaging with the world in prayer), Amazon.

Celtic Daily Prayer, Collins, 2005.

Information on Celtic festivals is taken mainly and unashamedly from Wikipedia.

Holy Bible, New International Version® Anglicized, NIV® Copyright © 1979, 1984, 2011 by Biblica, Inc.® Used by permission. All rights reserved worldwide.

About the Author

John Birch is a Methodist Local Preacher based in South Wales, and as well as self-publishing books of prayers and Bible studies, writes for IBRF daily study notes, created faithandworship.com (an online prayer resource) and has had prayers published in a range of denominational publications.

A book of around 700 of his prayers for the three year Lectionary cycle of readings is published by BRF (Bible Reading Fellowship) and available in Christian book shops and Amazon.

A collection of 300 prayers entitled "Ripples : Engaging with the world in prayer" is available in paperback from Amazon.

A variety of Bible study resources on Lent, Advent and some Celtic themes are available to purchase and download from www.faithandworship.com.

Made in United States
North Haven, CT
26 November 2021

11553774R00075